Bix Is Sick

by Shirley Horton

Scott Foresman
is an imprint of

Glenview, Illinois • Boston, Massachusetts • Mesa, Arizona
Shoreview, Minnesota • Upper Saddle River, New Jersey

Every effort has been made to secure permission and provide appropriate credit for photographic material. The publisher deeply regrets any omission and pledges to correct errors called to its attention in subsequent editions.

Unless otherwise acknowledged, all photographs are the property of Pearson.

Photo locations denoted as follows: Top (T), Center (C), Bottom (B), Left (L), Right (R), Background (Bkgd)

Opener © Dorling Kindersley; 1 © Dorling Kindersley; 2 © Dorling Kindersley; 3 © Dorling Kindersley; 4 © Dorling Kindersley; 5 © Dorling Kindersley; 6 © Dorling Kindersley; 8 © Dorling Kindersley

ISBN 13: 978-0-328-39287-2
ISBN 10: 0-328-39287-1

1 2 3 4 5 6 7 8 9 10 V010 17 16 15 14 13 12 11 10 09 08

Look at Bix.

Look at Bix in the van.

Look at Bix and the vet.

Look at Bix take the paper.

Look at Bix.
What can she do?

Medicine for Pets

Read Together

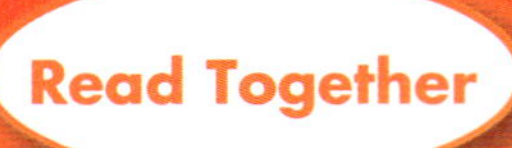

Some vets make medicine for pets. Dogs will take medicine that tastes like cheese. Cats will take medicine that tastes like fish. Birds will take medicine that tastes like fruit. What do you think medicine for rabbits tastes like?

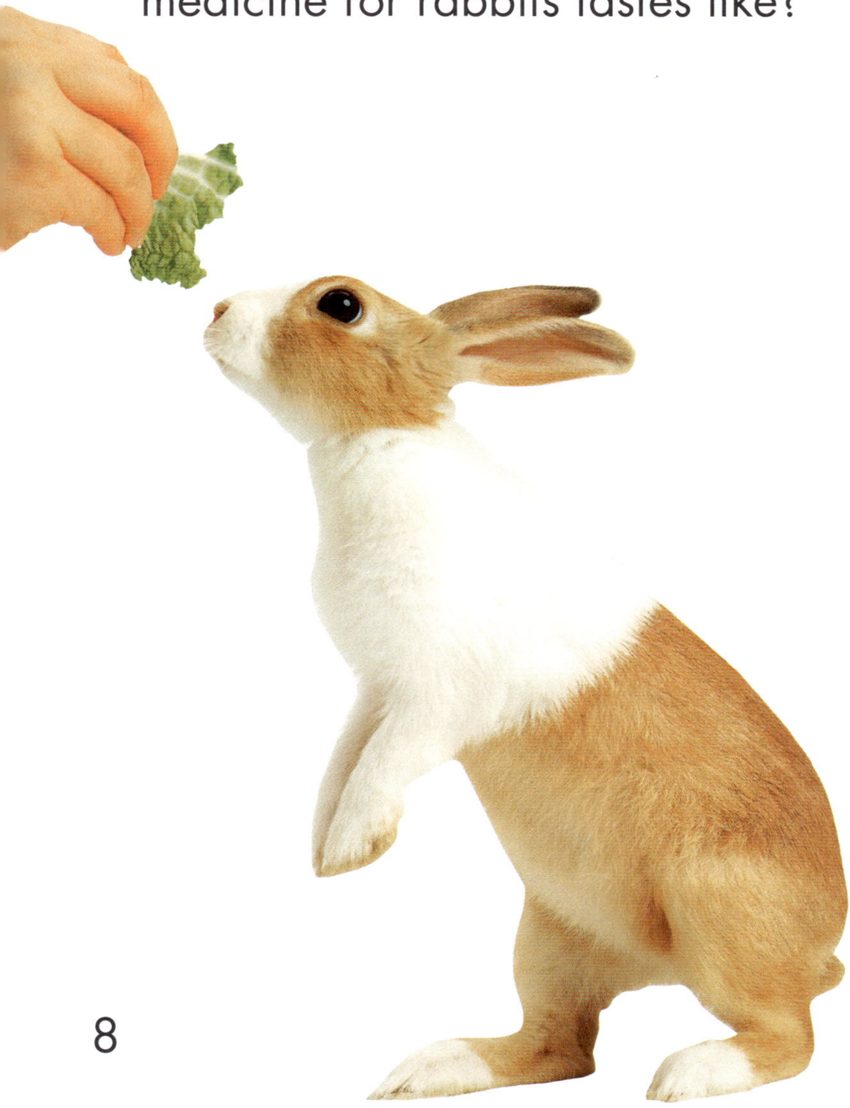